I0648264

Cordelia C. Nevers, Roberta H. Montgomery

Songs of Wellesley

Cordelia C. Nevers, Roberta H. Montgomery

Songs of Wellesley

ISBN/EAN: 9783743306875

Manufactured in Europe, USA, Canada, Australia, Japa

Cover: Foto ©Thomas Meinert / pixelio.de

Manufactured and distributed by brebook publishing software
(www.brebook.com)

Cordelia C. Nevers, Roberta H. Montgomery

Songs of Wellesley

SONGS

OF

WELLESLEY.

A COLLECTION OF SONGS FOR THE USE OF

THE

GLEE CLUB AND STUDENTS

OF

WELLESLEY COLLEGE.

COMPILED AND EDITED BY

CORDELIA C. NEVERS, '96,

AND

ROBERTA H. MONTGOMERY, '97.

PUBLISHED AT

WELLESLEY, MASS.

PREFACE.

For a long time there has been felt the lack of some means of becoming familiar with the songs of our College which all of us know about, but do not really know; and it is in the hope of meeting this deficiency, that this collection has been made.

It has been the aim of the editors to include all the Wellesley songs, written from time to time, which are worthy of preservation. In addition to the older and better known songs, the collection includes many of the later and less familiar ones, as well as some that have not appeared before; also a few general favorites, not of Wellesley origin, without which no college song book seems complete.

The editors wish to express their thanks for the cordial assistance they have received from many sources, and especially from leaders of the glee club. They also gratefully acknowledge the courtesy of the editors of '92 Legenda in permitting them to use the songs which first appeared in their publication.

ROBERTA H. MONTGOMERY.

CORDELIA C. NEVERS.

CONTENTS.

Songs of Wellesley.

ALL HAIL TO THE COLLEGE BEAUTIFUL.

KATHERINE LEE BATES.

C. H. MORSE.

Con moto.

SOPRANOS.

1. All hail to the Col - lege Beau - ti - ful! All hail to the Welles - ley
2. All hail to the Col - lege Beau - ti - ful! All hail to the brave and
3. All hail to the Col - lege Beau - ti - ful! All hail to the sa - cred

ALTOS.

blue! All hail to the girls who are gath'ring pearls From the shells that are o -
bright! She has taken her place in the swift-sandaled race, Where the strong man smiles
walls! Where, sinking a - way in the shad - ow - y gray, Aye, the sun's last ra -

p grazioso.

pen to few! From the shells up - cast by the ebb - ing Past On the
in his might, Oh! shining a - rise the lights in her eyes, And her
di - ance falls! Where first on the lake the day - beams a - wake, And the

p

Copyright, 1878, by C. H. Morse.

All Hail to the College Beautiful.

All Hail to the College Beautiful.

'NEATH THE OAKS.

Words and Music after 'Neath the Elms of Old Trinity.   Arr. by EDITH PINGREE SAWYER.

1. 'Neath the oaks of our old Welles - ley,   'Neath the oaks of our
2. On the hills of our old Welles - ley,   In the halls of our
3. College days are from care and sorrow free.   And oft will we
4. Then we'll sing to our old Welles - ley,   To our dear old Alma

dear old Welles - ley,   'Tis with pleas-ure we meet, Our old
dear old Welles - ley,   There is right mer - ry cheer, There are
seek in mem - o - ry.   The . . . days that are past, Far too
Ma - ter Welles - ley,   We're to-geth - er to - day, And to-

class-mates to greet, 'Neath the oaks of our old Welles - ley.
friends true and dear, In the halls of our old Welles - ley.
joy - ous to last, 'Neath the oaks of our old Welles - ley.
mor - row a - way, Far a - way from our old Welles - ley.

MY COLLEGE GIRL.

ALICE W. KELLOGG.   JUNIUS W. HILL.

Lively staccato.

1. She is skilled in math-e-matics, And knows more of hy-dro-stat-ics Than I
2. She can French and Ger-man speak, And can write in an-cient Greek, Getting
3. She, al-tho' 'tis not her habit, Can dis-sect a good sized rabbit, Giving

learned in all my plodding years at Yale. She performs ex-per-i-ments, With the
all the various accents quite cor-rect. Tho' she deals hard blows at Russians In his-
you the name of each and ev'-ry bone. Much she knows of plant and tree, On the

divers elements, That would make her little brother's cheek turn pale. She performs exper
tor-i-cal discussions, Not a flaw in all her log-ic I detect. Tho' she deals hard blows
land and in the sea, Slighting not meanwhile the all-important stone. Much she knows of plant

iments With the divers el-ements, That would make her little brother's cheek turn pale.
at Russians In historical discussions, Not a flaw in all her log-ic I de-tect.
and tree, On the land and in the sea, Slighting not meanwhile the all-im-port-ant stone.

4 Like a statue she can pose,
  And interpret learned prose,
In a way that makes my pulses wildly beat.
  She has studied poetry lyric,
  Epic also and satiric,
Till her diction and her style are quite complete.

5 More than all, the little sinner,
  She can cook as good a dinner
As a hungry man would ever wish to spy;
  And I challenge the world over
  If two folks they can discover
Quite so happy as my college girl and I.

A FACULTY TEA.

Arr'd. by F. BLUME.

1. The Fac - ul - ty, se - date and grave, A Fac - ul - ty re - cep - tion gave, To
2. A lone - ly few they are, 'tis true, And so lest they should stay a - way, Tell
3.

meet the dame from Smith who came, To size us up at Wel - les - ley. Said
all the five to bring their wives, A - long with them to Wel - les - ley." But
Which

they," we'll have sal - tines and tea, What glee! just see! 'twill be a spree, And
oh, a - las! it came to pass, That when the same to Wellesley came, Each
brings us to the mor - al true. Don't be too sure—'tis in - se - cure, Be

then a - gain, we'll ask the men Who cours - es give at Wel - les - ley.
begged to be ex - cused, that he No wife could bring to Wel - les - ley.
quite po - lite, but don't in - vite Hy - po - the - ses to Wel - les - ley.

CHORUS. *With feeling.*

Oh, the Fac - ul - ty! the Fac - ul - ty! the Fac - ul - ty!

Repeat Chorus. ff

Oh, the Fac - ul - ty! the Fac - ul - ty of Welles - ley.

JUANITA.

LOVE SONG.

JOSEPHINE PRICE SIMRALL.

SUE M. LUM.

1. Dearest, my heart is full of
2. Dearest, my heart is full of

love, But I can - not speak it to - day, ... For the light is
pain, But I hide it deep out of sight, ... For sun-shine is

gone from the sky a - bove, And the clouds are all dark and gray.
fill - ing the sky a - gain, And the world is a - glow with light.

CREW SONG.

ALICE W. KELLOGG.

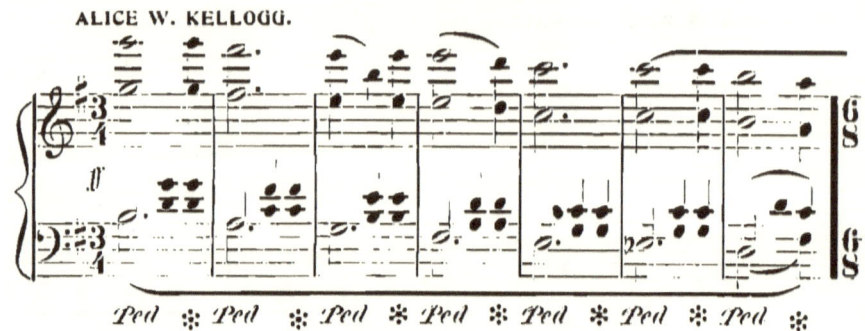

1. Breezes from Waban blow gent - - ly.
2. Swift-ly we move thro' the wa - - ters.
3. Home a-gain float we in si - - lence.

Daylight steals out of the sky,   Birds their sweet songs all are hush - ing,
Sil - ver foam leaps from the oar,   Farther and farther be - hind   us,
Silence un - broken by song,   For with each splash of the oar   dip,

Crew Song.

Shadows   of evening draw nigh,   Now in   our bark fair and
Leave we   the shad-ow - y   shore: Leave it,   but back thro' the
Mem - o - ries man - ifold   throng.   Farewell   now   to   the

state - - ly.   Float we   a - way and a - way:
still - - ness,   Mes - sage   of   mu - sic we   send,
breez - - es,   And moon   of   the silv - ery   light,

Ra - di - ant moonbeams and star - - - light, Guiding   our path with their ray,
That now with the rhythm of rip - - - ples, And now with the breezes doth blend,
Beau - ti - ful wa - ters of Wa - - - ban, Sad - ly   we   bid you good-night.

ALUMNAE SONG.

JOSEPHINE A. CASS.

1. Ours is the hap-py past! Sing we now, Soft and low, Sing for the
2. Ours, too, the pres-ent is, Ours with its joy and pain. Sing we a

days that go, Ne'er to re-turn! Swift tho' the years may fly,
min-gled strain, Each meeting each. Glad tho' our meet-ing be,

Clouds on a stormy blast, Safe as the fair, blue sky, Bid-eth our past.
Some fa-ces dear we miss; Sa-cred their mem-o-ry, In hour like this.

3 Ours are the future days!
  Ours for the stronger strife,
  Ours for the larger life,
    Helping the world!
O'er white fields looking out,
Joyous the song we raise;
Hope overmasters doubt,
    Welcome, bright days!

4 Ours is Eternity!
  Where Then and Now are one.
  All rivers under sun,
    Find here their home!
Tho' life seem incomplete,
Not far our dim eyes see;
Fragments ere long shall meet
    And perfect be.

H2 SO4.

MARY ENO RUSSELL.

1. *Directions.* You take a few pieces of zinc, And put in your gen-er-a-tor. Add
2. *Observations.* The ac-tion was not ver y brisk When I put in H2 S O 4, So I
3. *Conclusions.* As I wiped up the ac-id and zinc, And swept up the glass from the floor, I con -

CHORUS.

wa - ter, then plug in the cork, And pour in H 2 S O 4. And
tried nit - ric ac - id to see If the thing wouldn't bub - ble up more. If the
clud-ed I'd stick to directions, And try my own methods no more. And

pour in H 2 S O 4, And pour in H 2 S O 4; Add
thing wouldn't bub - ble up more, If the thing wouldn't bub - ble up more; So I
try my own methods no more, And try my own methods no more; I con -

wa - ter, then plug in the cork, And pour in H 2 S O 4.
tried ni - tric ac id to see If the thing wouldn't bub - ble up more.
clud-ed I'd stick to di - rections, And try my own methods no more.

LULLABY.

EMILY S. JOHNSON.

FRANCIS E. MASON.

1. Dreami - ly, dreami - ly swing - ing, swaying. Blow as the blos - soms blow,
2. Glee - ful-ly, dain - ti-ly swing - ing, swaying. Blossoms blow light in the wind;

Intended for Soprano Solo with Violin Obligato, Alto ad lib.
Copyright 1897 by R. H. Montgomery.

Lullaby.

Ba - be-kyn rocks in a fae - - ry cra - dle, Now . . . high, now
Dawn-tint-ed pet - als fall thickly, till ba - by Is . . . . hard to

low.   Ba - be-kyn rocks in a fae - - ry cra - dle,
find.   Wear - i - ly, wear - i - ly rock - - ing, sway - ing,

Lullaby.

Hung from the white moon's horn,
Ev - en the rob - ins nest:
Pil - lowed on cling - ing,
When the sun is dead and

shimmer - ing flee - es.
the blos - soms shiv - er,
From the bright clouds shorn......
Long.... dreams are best......

JOSEPHINE P. SIMRALL.   SUE M. LUM.

1. I found it ly - ing on the
2. Its beau-ty gone, its fra - grance

floor,— The rose I gave her yes - ter - day; The lit - tle flow'r she
sweet Spent all in vain up - on the air: I found it ly - ing

prized no more Than just to wear, then throw a - way.
at my feet Where it had fal - len from her hair.

TO PROFESSOR ——.

JOSEPH MOSENTHAL.

1. Good morrow, grave pro-fessor, now prythee tell me true; To be as wise as the

1. Good morrow, grave pro-fessor, now prythee tell me true; To be as wise as the

1. Good morrow, grave pro-fessor, now prythee tell me, tell me true; To be as wise as the

Fa-culty, what must a body do? To gain a Faculty cast of mind, a little girl like

Fa-culty, what must a body do? To gain a Faculty cast of mind, a little girl like

Fa-culty, what must a body do? To gain a Faculty cast of mind, a little, lit-tle

Copyright, 1885, by the Century Company.
Adapted from St Nicholas Songs, with permission of the publishers.

To Professor ——.

you   must grind and grind, and grind and grind, and that's what she must do, Just do.

you   must grind and grind, and grind and grind, and that's what she must do, Just do.

girl like you must grind and grind, and grind and grind,   that's what she must do, Just do.

2 " Now tell me, grave professor,
    And prythee tell me true ;
    To gain a Junior promenade,
    What must a body do ?"
" To gain a Junior promenade,
    The wisest course would be,
    To send a bunch of daffodils,
    Into the great A. C."

3 " O tell me, grave professor,
    And prythee tell me true ;
    To gain a Senior cap and gown,
    What must a Freshman do ?"
" A Senior cap and gown to gain,
    A little girl like you,
    Must work with all her might and main,
    And pass *with credit*, too."

4 " Now tell me, grave professor,
    Please tell me just once more,
    What do those words " *with credit*," mean ?
    It was not so of yore !"
" To make a record of C or more,
    The thing to carry you through,
    Is art in bluffing three times in four,
    So that's the game for you."

BOO! HOO!

Music from the " Sphinx," by LEWIS S. THOMPSON.

Music used by permission of MILES & THOMPSON, Boston, owners of right to Publish.

Boo! Hoo!

fill up all my day With En-glish, Greek and Lat - in, Math. and Gym.
make me dust and sweep A great, big, gloom- y room called P. L. R.
most for - got to say. There are some dread- ful girls called Soph - o - mores.

Oh! oh! and then they kindly say." Plenty time to *spatziergehen* in."
Oh! oh! they make me go to sleep. No matter how unlearned my lessons are.
Oh! oh! I heard my room-mate say That they were going to haze us. (What's that, Ma?

pp

dim molto.

Boo! hoo! Boo! hoo! Boo! hoo! hoo!
Boo! hoo! Boo! hoo! Boo! hoo! hoo!
Boo! hoo! Boo! hoo! Boo! hoo! hoo!

pp   *pp*   *pp*   *pp*

BOATING SONG.

KENT DUNLAP HÄGLER.

SUE M. LUM.

Marcato.

1. A - way! a - way! more fleet than thoughts can fol - low, Like a
2. A - way, a - way! we leave the task en - thrall - ing, Winds are
3. A - way, a - way! no thought of dull to - mor - row— Now we

swal - low flies our wing - ed boat a - long; In
call - ing morn is laugh - ing in the sky: Be -
bor - row mirth and free - dom from the day; Each

meas - ured stroke our strength the lithe oar bend - ing, Voic - es
fore our boat the blithe waves quick re - treat - ing, Tim - id
rest - less heart with calm and cour - age fill - ing, Hope in -

Boating Song.

blend - ing wake the ech - oes with our song.
greet - ing mur - mur as we hur - ry by.
still - ing glide the care - less hours a - - way.

REFRAIN.

Voic - es blend - ing with the waves in glad re - frain, . . . Voic - es

blend - ing wake the ech - oes with our strain.

WELLESLEY COLLEGE.

Wellesley College.

Oh. Welles - ley Col - lege, our Welles - ley Col - lege, Chief of all

oth - ers we crown thee as queen, Oh, Welles - ley Col - lege,

our Welles - ley College, Thy like 'mongst the na - tions nev - er was seen.

A HOBBY.

MABEL W. WHITE.

SUE M. LUM,

1. There is a sprightly maiden, We all know ver-y well, Who rides a pranc-
2. For dress reform she's striving, And more el-oquent is she, Than a-ny Dan-

ing hob-by Up-on which she loves to dwell. This hob-by is not learning, Tho' in
iel Webster, Or a Hen-ry Clay could be. If her dress should be constricting To her

that she does ex-cel, Nor yet the rights of woman, Which she upholds so well.
superhuman breath, She would cry with Patrick Henry, "Give me lib-er-ty or death."

SWEET AND LOW.

ALFRED TENNYSON.   J. BARNBY.

1. Sweet and low, sweet and low, Wind of the west - ern sea; Low, low,
2. Sleep and rest, sleep and rest, Fa - ther will come to thee soon; Rest, rest on

breathe and blow, Wind of the west - ern sea; O - ver the roll - ing
mother's breast, Fa - ther will come to thee soon; Fa - ther will come to his

wa - ters go, Come from the dy - ing moon and blow, Blow him a - gain to
babe in the nest, Sil - ver sails all out of the west, Un - der the sil - ver

me, While my lit - tle one, while my pret - ty one sleeps.
moon: Sleep, my lit - tle one, sleep, my pret - ty one, sleep.

INVITED BY MISTAKE.

SARAH J. McNARY.　　　　　　　　ROBERTA H. MONTGOMERY.

1. A cal-low youth received an in-vi-ta-tion to the Prom; He
2. A smil-ing ush-er brought him to a la-dy young and fair; Though
3. They wandered thro' the cor-ridors, and out be-neath the sky; He

scarce-ly was ac-quainted with the maid-en it was from; But
nei-ther e'er had seen the oth-er, what did ei-ther care? An
seemed a tri-fle spoon-y, and he heaved a pen-sive sigh. He

not the slightest dif'-rence did so small a mat-ter make Un-
in-tro-duc-tion might, thou't he, this rare en-joyment break; But
grew more sen-ti-men-tal as they neared the rip-pling lake; He

to this luck-less youth who was in-vit-ed by mis-take.
she full soon di-vined he was in-vit-ed by mis-take.
said the prop-er thing, al-though in-vit-ed by mis-take.

Invited by Mistake.

CHORUS.

He will nev-er for-get the ic-es, He will nev-er for-get the cake; But he'll

al-ways wish he had-n't been In-vit-ed by mis-take. He will

nev-er for-get the ic-es, He will nev-er for-get the cake; But he'll

al-ways wish he had-n't been In-vit-ed by mis-take.

4 Oh! artfully she led him on,—this fresh and verdant youth;
She took some friends into the plot, and fun they had in sooth.
He thought she was a freshman, and, accordingly, he spake
Abundant foolishness, this man invited by mistake.

5 Still funnier he grew, and eke, he did facetiously
Make jokes about our rules, and e'en the sacred faculty;
But when she said " Good night," her words with horror made him quake:
" I am Professor Blank; you were invited by mistake."

ETON BOATING SONG.

1. Jol - ly boat - ing weather, And a fresh June breeze;
2. Oh what mer - ry madness In each sparkling eye!

Blade on the feath - er, Shade on the trees.
Earth knows naught of sad - ness, Eve - ry heart beats high.

CHORUS.

Swing, swing to - geth - er, With your bod - y be - tween your knees,
Sing, sing for gladness, Let the hills and woods re - ply,

Swing, swing to - geth - er, With your body be - tween your knees.
Sing, sing for gladness, Let the woods and hills re - ply.

3 Others will soon replace us,
   Others will cheer the blue;
   But here's to those who love us,
   And here's to our jolly crew.
   ‖: May we ever be as happy
   When we paddle our own canoe.

4 Twenty years hence this weather
   Will bring us back to Float;
   From distant lands we'll gather,
   Be they ever so remote.
   ‖: Perhaps we'll forget to feather,
   But we'll manage to pull the boat.

A LULLABY.

JOSEPHINE SIMRALL,

p Dreamily.

SUE M. LUM,

1. Dream - i - ly, Dream - i - ly, to and fro, How - so -
2. The birds are twit - ter - ing low and high, A la - zy

ev - er the breez - es blow, Cast - ing soft shades on the
but - ter - fly flit - ting by, Has paused to list to the

grass be - low, The leaf - la - dened branch - es swing.
mel - o - dy Which the wan - d'ring breez - es sing.

'93 CREW SONG.

JOSEPHINE P. SIMRALL.　　　　　　　　　**LEWIS S. THOMPSON.**

All hap - pi - ly rowing, The shades, 'round us growing, Wrap us close in their

man-tle of rest; . . . . . The night mists surround us, Soft twi - light has

found us As we float up - on fair Wa - ban's breast. . . . . . All

Music used by permission of MILLS & THOMPSON, owners of Copyright.

'93 Crew Song.

mer - ri - ly sing - ing, With blithe ech - oes ring - ing, The hill - sides give

back the re - frain; . . . . . In re - sponse to our voi - ces Sweet Na - ture re -

FINE.

joi - ces, And flings back our mu - sic a - gain. (back a - gain.)

'93 Crew Song.

O - ver the beau-ti-ful wa - ters we go, And backward and

flit . . . . .

forward we flit to and fro; Sing-ing so blithely we ban-ish all

glad - - ness

sadness, As onward we row in - to Nature's pure glad-ness Soft ev'ning

shad-ows a-round us lie dreaming, But gold-en the light in our

path - - - way,

path-way is gleaming, For gold is the glow of the sun in his

D. C.

dy-ing, And golden the hours so swift in their fly-ing. All

LAKE WABAN.

LOUISE MANNING HODGKINS.

1. Lake of gray at dawn-ing day, In soft shad-ows ly-ing;
2. Lake of blue, a mer-ry crew, Cheer of thee would bor-row;
3. Lake of gold, with gems un-told, On thy bo-som glow-ing;
4. Lake of white at ho-ly night, In the moon-light gleaming;

cresc.

Wa-ters kissed by morn-ing mist, Ear-ly breez-es sigh-ing.
Hap-py hours to-day are ours, Weight-ed by no sor-row.
Pictures fair, in am-bient air, Through the sun-set show-ing.
Soft-ly o'er thy wood-ed shore Sil-ver radiance stream-ing.

Fai-ry vi-sion as Thou art, Soon thy fleet-ing charms depart:
Oth-er years may bring us tears, Oth-er days be full of fears:
When morn-ing hours are with the past, And memory's gaze is eastward cast.
On the wave-lets bear a-way, Ev-'ry care we've known to-day,

dim. *pp*

Ev-'ry grace that wins the heart, Like our youth is fly-ing.
On-ly hope the craft now steers, Cares are for the mor-row.
The gold-en time shall then outlast Each gift of thy bestow-ing.
Bring, on thy re-turn-ing way, Peace-ful, hap-py dream-ing.

By raising the lower clef one octave, this piece may be used as a four-part song for women's voices.

ANNE BARRETT HUGHES.

FLORA SMEALLIE WARD.

1. { To Al - ma Ma - ter. Wellesley's daughters, All to - geth - er join and sing. }
   { Thro' all her wealth of wood and wa - ters, Let your hap - py voic - es ring. }

2. { We'll sing her prais - es now and ev - er, Bless - ed fount of truth and love. }
   { Our heart's de-vo - tion, may it nev - er Faithless or un - worthy prove. }

In ev - 'ry changing mood we love her, Love her tow'rs and woods and
We'll give our lives and hopes to serve her, Humblest, high - est, no - blest—

lake, Oh, changeful sky, bend blue a - bove her! Wake, ye birds, your chorus wake!
all, A stainless name we will preserve her, An - swer to her ev' - ry call.

Reharmonized by the author, 1897.

Copyright, MDCCCXCVII, by FLORA SMEALLIE WARD.

OTHER ARRANGEMENTS.

E. T. CARTER.

1. Our life it is jol-ly, and

al-ways so gay; We work and we love in the spir-it of play, And

sometimes make other arrangements. We hate credit systems, non-credit notes too, And

all quite agree they're a bore thro' and thro', And we try to make other arrangements.

CHORUS.

Oth-er arrangements we must make, Dif-fer-ent measures we must take:

Other arrangements, dif-fer-ent measures, Other arrangements we must make.

2 If we flunk more than twice when we're Freshmen in College,
  They say we are stupid and lacking in knowledge.
    And we have to make other arrangements.
  As Seniors we quake very much, for you see,
  If we fail or fall short we don't get a degree,
    And then 'tis too late for arrangements. CHORUS.

3 Our College is Wellesley, our color is blue,
  Our course it is four years—some stay only two,
    Two engaged in some other arrangements.
  The foxey invited the goosey to tea,
  The goosey accepted—oh dear, oh dear me,—
    And straightway they made their arrangements. CHORUS.

CRADLE SONG.

CLARA HOVEY RAYMOND.

Andante tenderezza.

1. Rock - a - by, lul - la - by, bees in the clo - ver,
2. Rock - a - by, lul - la - by, bees in the clo - ver,
3. Rock - a - by, lul - la - by, dew on the clo - ver,

Croon - ing so drow - si - ly, and cry - ing so low,
Tears on the eyes that wa - ver and weep,
Dew on the eyes that will spar - kle at dawn.

Rock - a - by, lul - la - by, dear lit - tle ro - - ver!
Rock - a - by, lul - la - by, bend - ing it o - - ver!
Rock - a - by, lul - la - by, dear lit - tle ro - - ver!

Cradle Song.

Down in - to won - der - land, go,.... oh, go!
Down to the moth - er world, sleep,... oh, sleep!
In - to the stil - ly world gone,... oh, gone!

After last verse only.

dim. -

Down to the un - der - land go, oh, oh, go!
Down to the oth - - er world, sleep,... oh, sleep!
In - to the lil - - y world gone,... oh, gone! Down in to

8va.

ritard. - - - - - - - - - - -

wonderland, Down to the un - der - land. . . . .

GEORGE BIRTHINGTON'S WASHDAY.

FLORENCE E. HOMER.

1. There was a famous washing day, its ac - tion near the Hub; A Nation's raiment
2. "The time is come," said Birthington, "when wash we really must. For see our country's
3. The morning dawn'd, the washers came, the washing was begun; The steam rose high, nor

in the suds, a he - ro at the tub. Then come, ye loy - al pa - tri - ots, and
garments, how they're tram-pled in the dust; And Lib - er-ty's bright tu - nic is so
ceased to rise till clean - li - ness was won. And now, tho' good George Birthington is

list - en to my lay! I'll sing of good George Birthington on this, his washing day.
sad - ly soiled, I ween, That nothing but a washing day will make it bright and clean."
gone to his re-pose, The grateful country still recalls how well he washed her clothes.

HER SECOND DEGREE.

Words and Music by **FRANCES C. LANCE.**

1. She was a Wellesley Sen - ior; The time, Commencement day: The
4. A doz - en years have flit - ted; That Sen - ior, as my bride, Has

spot,—nor word nor wa - ter Shall e'er her trust be - tray; For
found the world less rug - ged Since trav'-ling by my side. Her

there a gracious future Stood forth in glory dress'd, And in the vision promised To
dearest work do - mestic Is for our children three; A - las, must I disclose it! *Man*-

Her Second Degree.

answer her behest, That self-same day I rose from earth, And poised in Harvard sky, I
kind means chiefly me! Tho' Wellesley has not called her yet, Nor will that I can see, The

ritenuto.   *After 4th verse only.*

promptly caught each winged tho't That fain would pass me by.
hand-maid still of Love's sweet will, She's won her second degree.   M.   A.

2.   Exultantly they carolled, These tho'ts that flew so high, "Farewell, O work domestic, I
3. "To this old rugged earth-ball I pledge my service here, Until the world remolded, Rolls

Her Second Degree.

leave thee here to die; I go to sweep the shadows From hu-man na-ture's sky, My
on a per-fect sphere, Then Al-ma Ma-ter proudly Shall call me to her side, And

poco rit.

life, my love, my freedom, No single heart can buy; A-lone I search the world for truth; I
say, "your greatness, daughter, Is as the o-cean wide; In token slight of deep regard, This

kneel at no man's feet; She raiseth none who kneels to one,—My be-ing stands com-plete."
parchment take from me,—Heart, soul, and mind, spent for making, shall win my second de-gree."

1. Nev - er broke a reg - u - la - tion; Nev - er told a lie;
2. Nev - er want to run or whis - tle, For 'tis not po - lite;
3. To my brothers once was ten - der, Will not be a - gain;

Nev - er want to have va - ca - tion—When I don't know why.
Nev - er make a wretch - ed fiz - zle— When I don't re - cite.
Nev - er name the oth - er gen - der, Save to say, A - men.

Al - ways love to go to sections, Love to go to bed: Nev-
When I meet a Har - vard student Nev - er stop to talk: Nev-
You may gath - er from these da - ta Just how good I be; I'm

er nib - ble sweet con - fec - tions—When I am not fed.
er take a step im - pru - dent—When I do not walk.
as proud of Al - ma Ma - ter As she is of me.

MENS SANA.

KATHERINE LEE BATES.   JUNIUS W. HILL.

1. 'Tis a lit-tle out of date, The col-lege girl to rate, As
2. When she roams the flow-'ry land, A bot-a-ny in hand, She
3. It may yet be ver-y true She wears the hos-en blue, And is
4. Crick-et, golf, and bas-ket ball, She plays them one and all, And

house-hold bric-a-brac of or-der plas-tic. But we're
still has val-ues pict-ur-esque and seen-ic; But how-
great-ly class-i-cal and math-e-mat-ic; And al-
drives the wheel with mo-tion en-er-get-ic; Cam-pus,

grat-i-fied to state, That her ten-den-cy of late, Is to
ev-er fair her phiz, Her great-est glo-ry is To be
though we bode ill luck To the man who calls her duck, She is
lake, and hill and hall, Ech-o to her breez-y call, Come and

Mens Sana.

be gym - nas - tic, nas - tic, nas - tic, nas - tic, Is to be gym - nas - tic.
cal - is - then - ic, then - ic. then - ic, then - ic, To be cal - is - then - ic.
cer - tain - ly a - quat - ic, quat - ic, quat - ic, Cer - tain - ly a - quat - ic,
be ath - let - ic, let - ic, let - ic, let - ic, Come and be ath - let - ic.

Sing it from Main to Main O! From At - lan-tic to far Pa - cif - ic,

Mens Sa - na in cor - por - e Sa - no, Makes Wellesley be - a - tif - ic,

tif - ic, tif - ic, tif - ic, Makes Wel - les - ley be - - a - tif - ic.

Sing it from Main to Main O! From At - lan-tic to far Pa - cif - ic,

Mens Sa - na in cor - por - e Sa - no, Makes Wellesley be - a - tif - ic,

tif - ic, tif - ic, tif - ic, Makes Wel - les - ley be - - a - tif - ic.

A PARTING SONG.

JOSEPHINE P. SIMRALL.   MENDELSSOHN.

1. Full swift the years have sped a - way, It comes at last— our
2. We bless thee for our life's rich gain, For all thy truth-taught
3. We bless thee for thy se - crets deep, Of lake and sky and

sad - dest day, Our part - - ing.   Oh,
joy and pain, At part - - ing.   For
wood- land sweep; No part - - ing.   Nor

Al - ma Ma - ter, Moth - er true, Our hearts are filled with
friendship's mes - sage glad and strong; Though life be short, yet
years, nor miles can steal a - way The glad - ness of our

love for you At part - ing,   At part - - ing.
love is long At part - ing,   At part - - ing.
mem - o - ry— So part - ing,   So part - - ing.

A Parting Song.

4. Our life song to thy no - ble strain

Sounds not in vain; Some glad, glad day we

come a - gain, So sing we now, Auf - wie - der - sehen, Auf-

wie - der - sehen, Auf - wie - der - sehen!

'96 CLASS SONG.

MARY HEFFERAN.

Andante.

1. O loud and clear on the banks o' Lake Wa - ban, We'll
2. O firm and strong on the wa - ters o' Wa - ban, We'll
3. O fair and pure on the banks o' Lake Wa - ban, Our
4. And may the sunshine and rains o' Lake Wa - ban, Fall

sing you a song that shall ring through the trees: For white and
pull with a will while the bright clouds a - bove, Look down and
bon - ny sweet rose turns its face to the light. O pur - est
kind - ly and gent - ly up - on our ain tree, Till its branch-

crimson our col - ors are fly - ing, And wav - ing and flutt'ring a -
re - flect, like the face of a lad - die. With - in the deep eyes o' the
of flow'rs, on our breast we will wear thee. A charm a - gainst e - vil, sae
es strong, and its fresh leaves that whisper, All mur - mur a promise o'

'96 Class Song.

way in the breeze. O, bravely, O, freely, now sing in your gladness, Un-
las - sie he loves. O, bravely, O, freely, now sing in your gladness, Un-
spot-less and white. O, bravely, O, freely, now sing in your gladness, Un-
what we shall be. O, bravely, O, freely, now sing in your gladness, Un-

til your ain crimson grows dim in the west; Sing, O sing, for your

class and your college, And be your ain sel', be your truest and best.

'97 CLASS SONG.

JULIA D. RANDALL.   From Gounod's Faust.

1. Thy dear groves and hills so green. Thy lake of
2. Like our flow - er, so full of light, Our yel - low

sun - lit, gold, We with lov - ing eyes have seen,
daf - fo - dil! May our lives be brave and bright,

And in lov - - ing hearts shall hold. So the
Full of sun - - shine and good will. Not con -

ol - - ive of the moss, ... The gold of au -
tent to muse and dream, . . . Swift ac - tion be

TO ALMA MATER.

ANNE BARRETT HUGHES.　　　　　　**FLORA SMEALLIE WARD.**

Moderato.

1. { To Al-ma Ma-ter, Wellesley's daughters, All to-geth-er join and sing. }
   { Thro' all her wealth of wood and wa-ters, Let your hap-py voic-es ring. }
2. { We'll sing her prais-es now and ev-er, Bless-ed fount of truth and love. }
   { Our heart's de-vo-tion, may it nev-er Faithless or un-wor-thy prove. }

In ev-'ry chang-ing mood we love her, Love her tow'rs and woods and
We'll give our lives and hopes to serve her, Humblest, high-est, no-blest—

lake. Oh, changeful sky, bend blue a-bove her! Wake, ye birds, your chorus wake!
all, A stainless name we will preserve her, Answer to her ev'-ry call.

'98 CLASS SONG.

AMELIA M. ELY.   PHILLIP J. DÜRINGER.

1. Oh Wellesley, hear our song, So loud it rings and long, For Al - ma
2. Ac - cept our cornflow'r blue, Our beech tree's sil - ver hue: The word of

Ma - ter true, For sil - ver and for blue; We sing thy praises ev - er
hope we say To guide us on our way, And keep us each thy faithful

glad - ly.   We love thy sa - cred walls, We lin - ger
daugh - ter.   May Nine - ty - eight be strong, To serve and

in thy halls, And leave thee sad - ly, And leave thee sad - ly.
wor - ship long. Her Al - ma Ma - ter, Dear Al - ma Ma - ter.

'99 CLASS SONG.

ANNA E. WOLFSON.
CLARA W. BROWN.

SOLO.

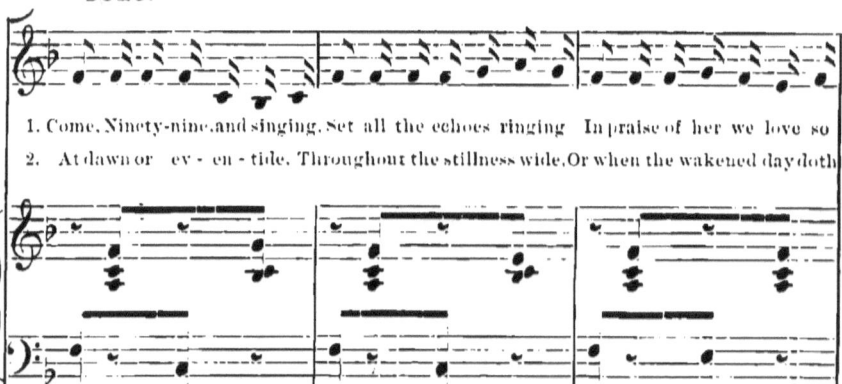

1. Come, Ninety-nine, and singing, Set all the echoes ringing In praise of her we love so
2. At dawn or ev - en - tide, Throughout the stillness wide, Or when the wakened day doth

true!   Steadfast, our Al - ma Ma - ter, Shall be thy loy - al daughter.
call.   Steadfast, our Al - ma Ma - ter, Shall be thy loy - al daughter,—

Faith - ful to Wellesley and the blue! . . . . Long hours of work and pleasure,
Stead - fast and faith - ful thro' all. . . . . When, the dear ser - vice end - ed,

Life filled to full - est measure. All these and more we owe to thee;
Mem - o - ries soft - ly blend - ed, Bring back this hap - py, golden day.

Bright be thy mem'ry ev - er. We can forget, no nev - er, Our Alma Mater, Our
Wilt thou, too, grant us dreaming Thy love in truth and seeming, Thy tender care o'er us

'99 Class Song.

Wellesley.
al - way.

CHORUS.

Welles - ley for - ev - er, ... Long   may she

Tempo di marcia.

live!   Loy - al   de - vo - - tion   to   her we give.

Thro' summer's green and winter's white, Nine - ty - nine shall be steadfast to

dear Welles - ley. . . . . Thro' summer's green and winter's white, Nine-ty-nine shall

be stead - - fast to dear Wellesley ley.

WELLESLEY MÄDCHEN.

Tune : — " JOHNNY SCHMOKER."

1 Wellesley Mädchen, Wellesley Mädchen,
Ich kann thun, Ich kann thun.
Ich kann thun and get to chapel,
||: Run, run, run, das ist get to chapel. :||

2 Wellesley Mädchen, Wellesley Mädchen,
Ich kann thun, Ich kann thun,
Ich kann thun mein kleine study.
||: Dig dig, dig, das ist mein study, :||
Mein run, run, run,
Mein dig, dig, dig,
Das ist mein Wellesley.

3 Wellesley Mädchen, Wellesley Mädchen,
Ich kann thun, Ich kann thun,
Ich kann thun mein Elocution.
||: Ah A - a - a - ah, das Elocution, :||
Mein run, run, run,
Mein dig, dig, dig,
Mein A - a - a - ah.
Das ist mein Wellesley.

4 Wellesley Mädchen, Wellesley Mädchen,
Ich kann thun, Ich kann thun,
Ich kann thun mein Swedish movements.
||: Forward, drop, das Swedish movement, :||
Mein run, run, run,
Mein &c. . . . . . .
Mein forward, drop,
Das ist mein Wellesley.

5 Wellesley Mädchen, Wellesley Mädchen,
Ich kann thun, Ich kann thun,
Ich kann thun right in mein half-shell,
||: Row, row, row, das ist mein half-shell. :||
Mein run, run, run,
Mein &c. . . . . . .
Mein row, row, row,
Das ist mein Wellesley.

6 Wellesley Mädchen, Wellesley Mädchen,
Ich kann thun, Ich kann thun,
Ich kann thun mein liebes Basket-Ball,
||: Win, win, win, das ist mein Basket-Ball. :||
Mein run, run, run,
Mein &c. . . . . . .
Mein win, win, win,
Das ist mein Wellesley.

7 Wellesley Mädchen, Wellesley Mädchen,
Ich kann thun, Ich kann thun,
Ich kann thun mein golfer linken,
||: Walk, walk, walk, das ist mein golfer. :||
Mein run, run, run,
Mein &c. . . . . . .
Mein walk, walk, walk,
Das ist mein Wellesley.

8 Wellesley Mädchen, Wellesley Mädchen,
Ich kann thun, Ich kann thun,
Ich kann thun mein class elections,
||: Talk, talk, talk, das class elections. :||
Mein run, run, run,
Mein &c. . . . . . .
Mein talk, talk, talk,
Das ist mein Wellesley.

9 Wellesley Mädchen, Wellesley Mädchen,
Ich kann thun, Ich kann thun,
Ich kann thun at mein Barn-swallows,
||: Ha! Ha! Ha! das ist Barn-swallows. :||
Mein run, run, run,
Mein &c. . . . . . .
Mein Ha! Ha! Ha!
Das ist mein Wellesley.

10 Wellesley Mädchen, Wellesley Mdächen,
Ich kann thun, Ich kann thun,
Ich kann thun mein serenade.
||: Doodle doodle doo, das serenade. :||
Mein run, run, run,
Mein &c. . . . . . .
Mein doodle, doodle doo,
Das ist mein Wellesley.

11 Wellesley Mädchen, Wellesley Mädchen,
Ich kann thun, Ich kann thun,
Ich kann thun mein Senior May-day,
||: Roll, roll, roll, das ist mein May-day. :||
Mein run, run, run,
Mein &c. . . . . . .
Mein roll, roll, roll,
Das ist mein Wellesley.

12 Wellesley Mädchen, Wellesley Mädchen,
Ich kann thun, Ich kann thun,
Ich kann thun mein college cheer,
||: Tra la, la. das college cheer. :||
Mein run, run, run,
Mein dig, dig, dig.
Mein A - a - a - ah.
Mein forward, drop.
Mein row, row, row.
Mein win, win, win.
Mein walk, walk, walk.
Mein talk, talk, talk.
Mein Ha! Ha! Ha!
Mein doodle, doodle doo.
Mein roll, roll, roll.
Mein tra la, la.
Das ist mein Wellesley.

1. Oh thou Tupelo! thou hast a certain magic charm; Oh thou Tupelo! thou hast a magic charm, A magic charm is thine, love, The charmer there is mine, love, Oh thou Tupelo! thou hast a certain magic charm, Oh thou Tupelo! thou hast a magic charm.

2 Oh thou Tupelo! thou hast the lake, and moon and stars,
    The moon and stars are thine, love,
    The sun that's there is mine, love,

3 Oh thou Tupelo! thou hast a rustic bench or two,
    A rustic bench is thine, love,
    The rustic on it mine, love,

4 Oh thou Tupelo! thou hast a gentle, balmy air,
    The balmy air is thine, love,
    The wealthy heir is mine, love.

5 Oh thou Tupelo! thou hast all things above, around,
    All things around are thine, love,
    Except the arm, that's mine, love.

6 Oh thou Tupelo! thou hast the power to leaf in Spring,
    To leaf in Spring is thine, love,
    To leave just now is mine, love.

*BINGO.

1. Here's to Wellesley College, drink her down! Here's to Wellesley College, drink her down! Here's to Wellesley College, For 'tis there you get your knowledge, Drink her down, drink her down, drink her down! down! down! Balm in Gil-e-ad, Gil-e-ad, Balm in Gil-e-ad, Gil-e-ad, Balm in Gil-e-ad! way down on the Bin-go farm, We won't go there an-y more, We

* The beverage used on this occasion is *Huyler's* Cocoa.

Bingo.

won't go there an-y more, We won't go there an-y more! 'Way

down on the Bin-go farm. Bin-go! Bin-go! Bin-go! Bin-go!

FINE. *Spoken.* D.C. to

Bin-go! Bin-go! 'Way down on the Bin-go farm. B! I! N! G! O!

2 Here's to '94, may she live forever more.
3 Here's to '95, may she ever live and thrive.
4 Here's to '96, they're a set of jolly bricks.
5 Here's to '97, for she's sure to go to heaven.
6 Here's to '98, for she's always up to date.
7 Here's to '99, may she ever live and shine.
9 Here's to 1900, let her praises loud be thundered.

AT WELLESLEY.

Tune :— NEVIN'S " IN WINTER."

1 On mornings I get up on time
And wait the early bell's sweet chime;
At night I go to bed so soon
It seems almost like afternoon.

2 I have to go to bed and see
My unlearned lessons waiting me;
And hear the grown up people all
Go stealing past me in the hall.

3 And does it not seem hard to you
That when I have so much to do;
And I should like to study—then
I have to go to bed at ten?

DRINK TO ME ONLY WITH THINE EYES.

1. Drink to me on - ly with thine eyes, and I will pledge with mine,
2. I sent thee late a ro - sy wreath, not so much hon - 'ring thee,

Or leave a kiss with - in the cup, and I'll not ask for wine; The
As giv - ing it a hope that there it could not with-ered be; But

thirst that from the soul doth rise, doth ask a drink di - vine, ...
thou there-on didst on - ly breathe, and send'st it back to me, ...

Drink to Me Only with Thine Eyes.

But might I of Jove's nec-tar sip, I would not change for thine, for thine.
Since when it grows and smells, I swear, not of it - self, but thee, but thee.

STARS OF THE SUMMER NIGHT.

SERENADE.

p Dolce.

1. Stars of the summer night, Far in yon a - zure deeps, Hide, hide your
2. Moon of the summer night, Far in you west - ern steeps, Sink, sink in

golden light. She sleeps, my la-dy sleeps, She sleeps, she sleeps, my la-dy sleeps.
sil - ver light. She sleeps, my la-dy sleeps, She sleeps, she sleeps, my la-dy sleeps.

3 Wind of the summer night,
   Where yonder woodbine creeps,
Fold, fold thy pinions light,
   She sleeps, my lady sleeps.

4 Dreams of the summer night,
   Tell her, her lover keeps
Watch, while in slumbers light
   She sleeps, my lady sleeps.

TAINTOR BROS.

By raising the lower clef one octave, this piece may be used as a four-part song for women's voices.

A CAPITAL SHIP.

Arranged for Women's voices by ROBERTA H. MONTGOMERY.

Solo.

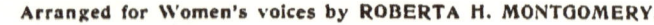

1. A capi-tal ship for an o-cean trip Was the walloping Window Blind! No

wind that blew dis-mayed her crew, Or troubled the captain's mind; The

man at the wheel was made to feel Con-tempt for the wildest blow-ow-ow, Tho' it

Copyright, MDCCCLXXXVI, by H. D. Sleeper.
Used by arrangement with Oliver Ditson Company, owners of the copyright.

A Capital Ship.

often appeared, when the gale had cleared, That he'd been in his bunk be - low.

CHORUS.

SOPRANO.

Then blow, ye winds, heigh-ho! A rov - ing I will go! I'll

1st ALTO.

Then blow, ye winds, heigh-ho! A rov - ing I will go! I'll

2d ALTO.

Then blow, ye winds, heigh-ho! A rov - ing I will go! I'll

Marcato.

A Capital Ship.

stay no more on England's shore, So let the mu-sic play-ay-ay! I'm

stay no more on England's shore, So let the mu-sic play-ay-ay! I'm

stay no more on England's shore, So let the mu-sic play-ay-ay! I'm

off for the morning train! I'll cross the rag-ing main! I'm

off for the morning train! I'll cross the rag-ing main! I'm

off for the morning train! I'll cross the rag-ing main! I'm

A Capital Ship.

off to my love with a box - ing glove, Ten thousand miles a - way.

off to my love with a box - ing glove, Ten thousand miles a - way.

off to my love with a box - ing glove, Ten thousand miles a - way.

2 The bo'swain's mate was very sedate,
  Yet fond of amusement too;
He played hop-scotch with the starboard watch,
  While the captain he tickled the crew!
And the gunner we had was apparently mad,
  For he sat on the after rai-ai-ail,
And fired salutes with the captain's boots,
  In the teeth of the booming gale!

3 The captain sat on the commodore's hat.
  And dined, in a royal way,
Off toasted pigs and pickles and figs,
  And gunnery bread each day;
And the cook was Dutch, and behaved as such;
  For the diet he gave the crew-ew-ew
Was a number of tons of hot cross-buns
  Served up with sugar and glue.

4 All nautical pride we laid aside,
  And we ran the vessel ashore
On the Gulliby Isles, where the Poopoo smiles,
  And the rubbly Ubdugs roar,
And we sat on the edge of a sandy ledge.
  And shot at the whistling bee-ee-ee.
And the cinnamon bats wore waterproof hats
  As they dipped in the shiny sea.

5 On Rugbug bark, from morn till dark.
  We dined till we all had grown
Uncommonly shrunk, when a Chinese junk
  Came up from the Torriby Zone.
She was chubby and square, but we didn't much care,
  So we cheerily put to sea-ee-ee:
And we left all the crew of the junk to chew
  On the bark of the Rugbug tree.

WHERE, O WHERE.

Spirited.

1. Where, O where are the verdant Freshmen? Where, O where are the verdant Freshmen?

Where, O where are the ver - dant Fresh - men? Safe now in the Soph'more Class.

They've gone out from their Mathematics, They've gone out from their Mathematics,

They've gone out from their Mathe - mat - ics, Safe now in the Soph'more Class.

2 ‖: Where, O where are the gay young Soph'mores? :‖
　Safe now in the Junior Class.
　‖: They've gone out from their Kings of Israel, :‖
　Safe now in the Junior Class.

3 ‖: Where, O where are the jolly Juniors? :‖
　Safe now in the Senior Class.
　‖: They've gone out from their three forensics, :‖
　Safe now in the Senior Class.

4 ‖: Where, O where are the grand old Seniors? :‖
　Safe now in the wide, wide world.
　‖: They've gone out from their Alma Mater, :‖
　Safe now in the wide, wide world.

5 ‖: Where, O where are the staid Alumnæ? :‖
　Lost, lost in the wide, wide world.
　‖: They've gone out from their dreams and theories, :‖
　Atoms lost in the wide, wide world.

RAY.	Specialties for	BELTS.
509	**Ladies**	ENGLISH HARNESS.
	"Viennese"	SPANISH BUCKLE.
WASHINGTON ST.,	Waists	TAKE POINT. (Just out.)
Corner of West	(Fisk, Clark & Flagg, Makers.)	STOCK CRAVATS,
Opp. R. H. White Co.	Silk, Satin,	TIES,
BOSTON.	Lace Brocade,	COLLARS and CUFFS,
	Madras,	
	Flannel.	UMBRELLAS.

J. G. SMALL & Co.

Ladies Fine Tailor-made Gowns, Dress Skirts, Bicycle Suits, Jackets, Capes and Shirt Waists.

Special Bargain

Tailor-made Suits in Canvas, Cheviot and Etamine cloths in all the latest shades, Skirt and Coat lined throughout with plain and fancy silk.   From $ 10.00 to $ 25.00

NO EXTRA CHARGE FOR SPECIAL ORDERS.

J. G. Small & Company,
542 Washington Street.
Opposite Keith's Theatre.

COMPREHENSIVE IN PLAN, Moderate in Price, Thorough in Practice, Famous for Results, with a corps of Teachers who are MASTERS IN THEIR SPECIAL DEPARTMENTS, the

New England
Conservatory
of Music
(Founded 1853 by Dr. E. Tourjee)

offers unequalled advantages to students seeking Thorough Instruction in Music, Musical Composition, and Elocution.

G. W. CHADWICK, Musical Director

SCHOOL YEAR BEGINS SEPTEMBER, 9.   Prospectus Free,

Address FRANK W. HALE, General Manager,
FRANKLIN SQUARE, BOSTON, MASS.,

Fine Gold Fraternity
Pins and Rings
Emblems, Jewels
Prize medals &c. &c.

Designed and Made by

HENRY C. HASKELL

11 John St., New York.

Design plates

sent upon request.

Union

Teachers' Bureau,

No. 1 Beacon Street,

Boston, Mass.

New system.

Positions guaranteed.

Correspondents in all parts of the United States.

Write for circulars and terms.

INTERCOLLEGIATE BUREAU

Cotrell & Leonard

472 & 474 Broadway,
ALBANY, N. Y.

Makers of the CAPS, GOWNS and HOODS
to the American Colleges, including Harvard,
Yale, Princeton, Columbia, Johns Hopkins,
Chicago, Wellesley, Bryn Mawr, Radcliffe,
Holyoke, Baltimore, etc.

Gowns for the Pulpit and the Bench.

Illustrated monograph, Samples etc. upon
application. Class contracts a specialty.

YOUNG LADIES SUITS
A SPECIALTY.

DISCOUNTS TO
STUDENTS & TEACHERS
OF
WELLESLEY COLLEGE.

" Make Assurance Doubly Sure."

The Equitable Life Assurance
Society of the United States

issues policies which combine in a high degree the advantages of Insurance and Investment.

To no class in the community is Life Insurance better adapted and more necessary than to those in

PROFESSIONAL LIFE.

It provides for the vicissitudes of death and those of old age. Among the patrons of the EQUITABLE are many of the

OFFICERS, PROFESSORS and STUDENTS

of our American Colleges including WELLESLEY.

The Guaranteed Cash Value policies both on the Life or En= dowment plans offer special attractions.

A small annual payment for a term of years furnishes an ab= solute guarantee for the future.

The Equitable is the best, safest and strongest Life Insurance Company in the world.

Correspondence solicited; Information and rates furnished.

Boston Office : EQUITABLE BUILDING,
Corner of Milk and Devonshire Streets.

NATHAN WARREN, Resident Secretary.

THE MATCHLESS

⋺| SHAW PIANO |⋲

BOYLSTON PIANO CO.

New England Representatives

• • • • • • •

FRANKLIN A. SHAW, Manager.

• • • • • • •

150 BOYLSTON STREET, - - - BOSTON.

Call or Send for Handsome Illustrated Catalogue.

LOUISE RYAN

Importer and Designer of

MILLINERY

Round Hats a Specialty.

110 Boylston Street.

Geo. P. Staples & Co.

INCORPORATED

•• Furniture & Carpets

739 Washington Street,

Cor. Dix Place, Boston.

TELEPHONE TREMONT 13

Boston's New Store

HIGH CLASS MILLINERY

— • ♦ ♦ • —

Where we are prepared to show special display of the latest creations in Hats and Bonnets for the spring and summer Season, including many exclusive designs of our own importation.

• • ♦ ♦ • •

Special attention paid to Wellesley College Pupils.

L. H. MELVILLE, = 161 TREMONT STREET.

SHALL I TELL YOU OF MY LOVER?

FRANCIS E. MASON.

Shall I tell you of my lov-er, brave and true? All his hidden charms discov-er to your view? Shall I tell you of his sweetness, Of his rich and full completeness? But I can't un-til I meet him: Now could you?

"WELLESLEY LYRICS, with a frontispiece, which shows the main college, the hill covered with trees, and suggests the charms of the lake, is made up of poems written by students and graduates of the College, with an introduction by Mrs. Alice Freeman Palmer. In her introduction Mrs. Palmer notes the fact that the college is not only a place for the acquisition of knowledge, but it is also a place where life is maturing, friendships forming, and youth, with its hopes, emotions, and experiences, has the field. It is out of this side of college life that these poems grew. It is an expression of the social and intellectual life of the College that the selection finds its chief value, and he must be hard to please who will not find in this volume evidences of the good fellowship, the fine feeling, the high sense of duty, and the generous aspiration which characterize the College whose name appears on the title-page of this volume." *The Outlook.*

Christmas Edition Bound in White and Gold, New Edition in Olive Green and Gold.
$1.00. Post-paid, $1.10. Gilt Top, post-paid, $1.25.
Address. CORDELIA C. NEVERS. Wellesley, Mass.

BON MARCHÉ

Rich · Millinery

OUR imported Hats, Toques and Bonnets, with those of our own exclusive designs, will excel all previous seasons, and will be placed at the . . .

° ° Reasonable Prices

for which we are noted. We invite you to an early inspection, feeling confident you will find designs that will interest you. . . .

Latest Novelties in Laces, Ribbons, Flowers, Straw Braids, Walking Hats, and Untrimmed Shapes. . .

451 Washington St., Opp. Shuman's.

FRANCIS WILSON
Proprietor.

H. Crine, The Furrier

15 and 17 AVON STREET

Announces the opening of a

LADIES' TAILORING DEPARTMENT

where he is prepared to make high class Costumes at very low prices.

Fur Garments made to order from selected skins, also your Furs re-dyed, repaired and altered.

No charge for storage when Furs are repaired.

Complete line of
SHIRT WAISTS

H. CRINE, THE FURRIER,
15 and 17 AVON ST

LOWELL BROS. & BAILEY,

GENERAL COMMISSION MERCHANTS
AND WHOLESALE DEALERS IN

Foreign and Domestic Fruits

AND PRODUCE OF ALL KINDS.

Nos. 73 and 75 Clinton St., Boston, Mass.

JOSEPH Q. LOWELL.
OSMON C. BAILEY.

REFERENCE: Fourth National Bank.
Boston Fruit and Produce Exchange.

The Lincoln St. Art Store,

GEO. D. MEARS, Mgr.

Pictures and Framing

Of every description.

182 Lincoln St., Boston Mass.

Old stand for 15 years,   Near B. & A. Depot.

20% discount to Wellesley College Students and Faculty.

J. Tailby & Son. FLORISTS,

Opposite Railroad Station,   Wellesley, Mass.

Flowers and Plants of the choicest varieties for all occasions ;

Palms, etc., to let for decoration. { FLOWERS carefully packed and forwarded by Mail or Express to all parts of the United States and Canada.

Orders by Mail or otherwise promptly attended to.   *Connected by Telephone.*

MR. JUNIUS W. HILL,

FOR THE PAST THIRTEEN YEARS

Director of the Wellesley College School of Music,

Will, after the close of this college year, devote himself entirely
to Private Instruction at his Studio in Boston,

154 TREMONT STREET.

SPECIALTIES. The art of Piano-playing, Organ, Harmony and
Voice Culture.   CORRESPONDENCE SOLICITED.
CIRCULARS SENT ON APPLICATION to any address.

The Dana Hall School   Wellesley, Mass.

Pupils are prepared for regular or for special courses at
Wellesley College.

Price for Board and Tuition, $500 for school year ;
Tuition for day pupils, $125.

The certificate admits to Wellesley College.

An early application necessary for admission.

For further information address the Principals :

Julia A. Eastman,
Sarah P. Eastman.

GOOD NIGHT, LADIES!

Good night, la - dies! Good night, la - dies! Good night, la - dies! We're

CHORUS.

going to leave you now. Mer - ri - ly we roll a - long, roll a - long,

roll a - long, Mer - ri - ly we roll a - long, o'er the dark blue sea.

2 Farewell, ladies, etc.   3 Sweet dreams, ladies, etc.

FOR LADIES

"The Shuman Corner Waist,"

$1.50 to $3.50,

In French Ginghams and Linens, Lappets, Nainsooks, Grass Cloths, Muslins, Trinities, Batistes, etc.

BELTS, TIES and STOCKS,

Bicycle Suits, Eton, Plain, Tight=fitting Coat and Half Tight= fitting Coat Styles; Bloomers, Golf Suits, Leggins, Sweaters, Bicycle Hats, Mackintoshes, English Walking and Sailor Hats, Shoes, etc.

A, Shuman & Company,

Shuman Corner   **WASHINGTON & SUMMER STS.**
BOSTON.

C. F. HOVEY & CO.

NOS. 33 SUMMER AND 42 AVON STREET, BOSTON.

◆◆　◆◆　◆◆

IMPORTERS AND RETAILERS OF

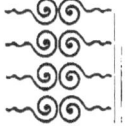 *Silks, Dress Goods, Trimmings, Cloaks, Suits and Ladies' Underwear.*

◆◆　◆◆　◆◆

ALL PURCHASES DELIVERED FREE AT WELLESLEY.

WHITNEY'S

Theadquarters for

Ladies'

All Linen

Handkerchiefs

WHITNEY'S

Temple Place, Boston.

SHOES

:x: AN IMPORTANT ITEM.

Where to get them

:x: ALSO IMPORTANT.

At Tuttle's . .

The latest, most approved styles are now on exhibition . . .

GOLF, BICYCLE, TENNIS STREET AND PARTY BOOTS AND SHOES.

:x: :x: Discount to Students

Henry H. Tuttle & Co.,

Washington & Winter Sts.,

Boston.

Ask Your Grocer

.. FOR ..

SWANSDOWN FLOUR ——

.. The Best Bread-Maker ..

H. S. BEAN.   H. H. KENDALL.

Conant & Bean

COMMISSION MERCHANTS

.. AND DEALERS IN .

Fruit · and · Produce

15 North Side Faneuil Hall Market,

.. BOSTON ..

A. J. ADAMS.   FRED. P. VIRGIN.   CHAS. G. BURGESS.

Martin L. Hall & Co.,

Wholesale Grocers,

13 and 14 SOUTH MARKET,

33 and 34 CHATHAM ST.,

 BOSTON.

ALWAYS INQUIRE FOR

Hildreth's Original and Only

Molasses Candy

America's Favorite,

THIS IS THE HOME OF THE VELVET.

THE LARGEST MOLASSES CANDY FACTORY
IN THE WORLD.

38 to 48 Batterymarch Street, Boston, Mass.

IT WILL PAY YOU TO EXAMINE

The most complete line of

BICYCLES IN BOSTON

Before purchasing elsewhere.

The " Park Flyer " = = = = = = =				$30.00
Crawfords = = = =		$37.50	$45.00	$50.00
B. & D. Specials = =		$75.00	$85.00	$100.00
Worlds = = = = = = = = = = =				$100.00
Tandems = = = =	$100.00	$135.00	$150.00

Boylston Cycle Company

390 Boylston Street, Boston.

Telephone 84 Tremont.

N. B. We advertise with those who patronize us.

Finest Roadbed on the Continent.

Through Car Line

Boston to The West

And Via. Springfield Line to

NEW YORK.

Drawing Room Cars on Day Trains.

Sleeping Cars on Night Trains.

For Time Tables, Space in Sleeping Cars, or Information
of any kind, apply to the nearest Ticket Agent, or

A. S. HANSON,
General Passenger Agent,
BOSTON, MASS.

FOR LUNCHEON,

RECEPTIONS,

AND TEAS

Kennedy's

(Salted or Unsalted.)

✳ Crisp

✳ Dainty

✳ Perfectly Baked

✳ and Beyond Criticism

◄ In Handsome One Pound Packages or in Bulk ►

Manufactured by

The New York Biscuit Company.

Sturtevant & Haley
Beef and Supply Company,

WHOLESALE AND RETAIL DEALERS IN

BEEF, PORK, LARD & HAMS.

ALSO

Fine Oleo Oil, Tallow & Stearine.

38 & 40 Faneuil Hall Market, Boston, Mass.

FACTORY AT 52 Somerville Ave., Somerville, Mass.
TELEPHONE CONNECTION.

Cobb, Bates & Yerxa Co.,

WHOLESALE AND RETAIL

8 Faneuil Hall Square,

BOSTON.

M. N. COBB.
H. D. YERXA.

J. P. BATES.
I. W. JOUETT.
J. N. PARKER.

OLIVER BROS.

SOUTH AVE.

NATICK, MASS.

Dealers in
LITTLE NECK CLAMS,
BLUE FISH, SAMON,
MACKEREL,
GREEN TURTLES,
SOFT SHELL CRABS,
SHRIMPS, CHICKEN HALLI=
BUT and all other kinds of fine
Sea Food Fish of every discription.

FREE DELIVERY In Wellesley Tuesday, Thursday and Saturday,

Agnes G. Downs,

MILLINERY,

24 South Main Street,

Natick, Mass.

SQUIRE'S
PURE
LEAF
LARD.

Little-Rendered.   Carefully and Cleanly Prepared.

Good Lard Makes Good Food.

Good cooks everywhere use SQUIRE'S
PURE LEAF LARD because it is PURE and
gives the best satisfaction. Better than any
patent substitute. Housekeepers buy it because it's more economical.

If it's SQUIRE'S, it's Pure.

JOHN P. SQUIRE & CO.,
BOSTON, MASS.

O. A. BROWN.

Family Bread,
Cake and Pastry,
Ice Cream and
Wedding Cake
AT SHORT NOTICE.

21 South Main Street,
Oposite Common.

NATICK, MASS.

Cambridge Edition of Famous Poets

COMPRISING IN ONE SINGLE VOLUME

The COMPLETE POETICAL WORKS of

JAMES RUSSELL LOWELL
HENRY WADSWORTH LONGFELLOW
JOHN GREENLEAF WHITTIER
OLIVER WENDELL HOLMES   ROBERT BROWNING

Each contains a fine portrait of the author and an engraved title=page, generally with a vignette of the poet's home. All have biographical sketches specially prepared for this edition, notes, in= dexes, etc. Each 8vo, printed and bound in the best style.

Price (except Browning) each—cloth, gilt top, $2.00; half calf, gilt top, $3.50; tree calf or full levant, $5.50. Browning, cloth, gilt top, $3.00; half calf, gilt top, $5.00; tree calf, or full levant, $7.00.

" The Cambridge Edition of the Great Poets is growing into a library which, when fin-ished, will leave little to be desired by those who wish to possess the master singers of the world, each in a single volume of the handsomest and most convenient typography, ac-companied by the most affluent materials for critical study and illustrative illumination of the text."—*Literary World*, BOSTON.

SOLD BY ALL BOOKSELLERS. SENT, POSTPAID, BY

HOUGHTON, MIFFLIN & CO., Boston.

M. A. Bailey,
Hats, Bonnets.
and
Millinery Goods.

887 WASHINGTON STREET,
BOSTON.

ISAAC LOCKE & Co.,
97, 99 & 101 Faneuil Hall Market,
BOSTON, MASS.

Wholesale and Retail Dealers in

FRUITS, VEGETABLES,
HOT-HOUSE PRODUCTS
and CANNED GOODS.

SPECIAL ATTENSION GIVEN
HOTEL, CLUB and FAMILY ORDERS.

Careful attention given to orders by
MAIL OR TELEPHONE.

COOK'S LADIES' LUNCH ☺☺☺ ☺☺

.AVON STREET ✄ ✄ ✄ IN THE MIDST OF THE SHOPPING DISTRICT

.... Where you will find Dainty, Palatable, and Nutritious food for moderate prices,

.... In our Catering Department, we give careful attention to the service of Class Day Spreads, Private Receptions, Dinners and Lunches.

... We have the largest facilities, most complete equipment, and the highest grade of goods, carefully prepared,

.... Orders for Ices or any article pertaining to dessert forwarded to any address,

JOEL GOLDTHWAIT & CO., ✄

━CARPETS━

.,169 Washington St,, Boston,

THE HORACE PARTRIDGE CO.━━━━

.. Bicycles and Games ..

LADIES' WHEELS A SPECIALTY.   We are Sole Agents for the

CYCLES. Royal Worcester, Halladay, Mercury, Middleton, Massasoit, Beebe

PRICES, $45 to $100

WE SOLICIT AN INSPECTION OF OUR LINE.

THE HORACE PARTRIDGE CO., 55 AND 57 HANOVER STREET, BOSTON.

Superior Moist Water Colors ☺☺ ☺☺

In Tubes, Pans and Half Pans. OIL COLORS in Tubes Manufactured expressly for Artists and Students' use, also

Drafting Instruments:

Drawing Papers, Sketching Easels and Outfits, and

Artists' Supplies

Of every description,

WADSWORTH, HOWLAND & CO., Incorporated

82 and 84 WASHINGTON STREET,   Factories, Malden, Mass.

www.ingramcontent.com/pod-product-compliance
Lightning Source LLC
Chambersburg PA
CBHW020033030726
47499CB00007B/2411